Transport

Mark Lambert

Wayland

Titles in this series

Art
Cinema
Communications
Fashion
Farming
Medicine
Transport
Warfare

Series Editor: Francesca Motisi
Editor: Jannet King
Series Designer: Charles Harford HSD
Designer: Ross George

Front cover *The dockland's railway, London.*
Back cover *A New York street in the 1920s.*
Title page *An illustration from the 1930s showing some of the uses to which petrol can be put.*

First published in 1989 by
Wayland (Publishers) Ltd
61 Western Road, Hove
East Sussex BN3 1JD, England

British Library Cataloguing in Publication Data
Lambert, Mark, 1946–
Twentieth century transport – (The twentieth century)
1. Transport, to 1980 – For children
I. Title   II. Series
380.5'09

ISBN 0–85078–926–5

Typeset by Kalligraphics Ltd, Horley, Surrey, England
Printed by G. Canale and C.S.p.A., Turin, Italy
Bound by Casterman, S.A., Belgium

Contents

1900–1913 Early Days — 4

The dawn of the motoring age — 4
Expansion of the railways — 8
Steam power at sea — 9
Into the air — 10

1914–1918 The Great War — 12

Land transport — 12
War at sea and in the air — 14

1919–1938 Between the Wars — 16

Motoring for all — 16
Railways — 18
Passenger transport in the air — 20
Carriers, diesel engines and hydrofoils — 22

1939–1945 The Second World War — 24

War on land — 24
War at sea — 26
War in the air — 28

1946–1956 The Jet Age — 30

Jet aircraft — 30
Specialist ships — 32
Postwar cars — 33
Postwar railways — 35

1957–1980 The Space Age — 36

Air travel for all — 38
Giant ships and nuclear power — 40
Family cars and high-speed trains — 42

1980–1990 Shuttles and Robots — 44

Glossary — 46

Further Reading — 47

Index — 48

Early Days

The history of transport began about 5,000 years ago and so, by 1900, many modern forms of transport were well established, but in the period before the First World War, dramatic changes occurred. The development of the internal combustion engine revolutionized land transport and enabled people to master another element — the air.

Above *One of the earliest forms of transport for both people and goods was animals.*

Since the dawn of history people have needed to move things from one place to another. Transport was first used thousands of years ago, when people began to use animals and boats to carry their belongings. Transport rapidly became an essential part of people's lives, and by the beginning of the twentieth century there were already many different ways of travelling. Ships and carriages were familiar means of getting from place to place, and the railway age was already well established. However, land transport was about to be revolutionized by the motorcar, and the age of the aeroplane was about to begin.

The dawn of the motoring age

In 1900, the horse and carriage was still a popular means of transport. However, the new horseless carriage, powered by the internal combustion engine, was now beginning to compete. During the 1880s, two German engineers, Gottlieb Daimler and Karl Benz had, independently of one another, started to produce successful four-stroke petrol engines. Benz was the first to see the commercial possibilities of using such engines in road vehicles, and he built his first three-wheeled car in 1885. A year later, Daimler tried out an engine in a phaeton carriage. In 1888, Benz began selling motorcars to the general public, and in 1895 Daimler was doing the same.

In March 1900, Daimler launched the first of the large, expensive cars, the Mercedes, but by this time Daimler and Benz were not alone. Car manufacturers operating at the turn of the century included Panhard and Levassor, Peugeot, Renault and De Dion Bouton in France, Duryea in the USA and Lanchester in Britain. All the basic features of modern cars had already appeared.

Left The Brougham, named after its designer, Lord Chancellor Brougham, was a horse-drawn street carriage, popular in England from 1838 until the early 1900s. This example was photographed in 1895.

Below Gottlieb Daimler (third from the left) in an 1891 Daimler, being driven by his design engineer Wilhelm Maybach. The engine is underneath the driver, who steers with a steering handle rather than a wheel. Notice that the passengers face the driver, who has to peer between them in order to see where he is going.

Engines were at the front rather than underneath, the steering wheel had replaced the steering lever, there were gears for providing different forward speeds and the wheels had pneumatic (air-filled) tyres. Other refinements included shaft instead of chain drive, multicylinder engines, the honeycomb radiator and the float-type carburettor.

In the early 1900s many manufacturers, such as Austin, Morris, Napier and Rolls-Royce started their companies. The motorcar was now no longer just a novelty; it was rapidly becoming a serious method of transport. One of the best-known cars built at that time was the Rolls-Royce 'Silver Ghost', which stayed in production from 1906 until 1925. As well as cars, petrol-driven motorcycles, lorries and buses were starting to be produced. In Britain, an early bus was known as the charabanc. This was a form of transport used by all but the rich, as motorcars were still very expensive.

In Europe, cheap vehicles, called cycle-cars, were popular for a short time, but in

Above A Vanguard bus about to start its daily journey from London to Brighton in 1905.

Right A 1911 version of the Model T Ford, or 'Tin Lizzie'.

the USA in 1908, Henry Ford introduced the Model T Ford, or 'Tin Lizzie'. This was a basic but well-built car, at a price many people could afford. It was the first car to be mass-produced and in 1909 the factory was producing 2,000 cars a month. In 1913, the assembly process was speeded up by the introduction of a moving assembly line. When the factory closed in 1927, over 15 million Model T Fords had been produced.

Expansion of the railways

The railways had been developed from the early 1800s. By 1900, they had become the most important form of transport available, and were continuing to expand rapidly throughout the world. Railway gauges (the distance between the rails) were becoming more standardized, 1,435 mm being the most common. The modern style of long passenger coach on two independent trucks, or bogies, had been developed in the USA. It had first been used in Britain in 1874, and was by now common throughout Europe.

The design of the steam locomotive had reached its peak by the 1900s. The basic design of locomotive, with horizontal pistons and a long boiler supported on several pairs of wheels, was now well established. The main change that took place during the first half of the twentieth century was an increase in size. The development of the first of the huge articulated Mallet and Garatt locomotives (weighing over 30 tonnes) took place in the early 1900s. Electric railways had been in use on underground lines in Britain since 1890, and the first diesel locomotive ran in Germany in 1912.

Below *Paddington Station, London, in 1912. Two G.W.R. 'Castle' 4-6-0 steam locomotives wait as passengers board two special trains for the King's Garden Party.*

Steam power at sea

At the turn of the century, steam was also the main form of power for ships. In 1884, the British inventor Sir Charles Parsons invented the steam turbine, which uses steam to turn a set of blades on a shaft. This is a much more efficient way of transferring power to a propeller shaft than the old method of using pistons to turn a crankshaft. As a result, ships could travel at greater speeds. After a demonstration in 1897, the world's navies and commercial shipping companies started using turbine power. The first diesel ship was the Russian tanker *Vandal* which was built in 1904.

Larger and larger ships were being built. The *Celtic*, produced in 1901 by the White Star Line, was the first ship to weigh more than 20,000 tonnes. Among other great liners of this time were the *Kronprinzessin Cecilie*, the *Kaiser Wilhelm II* (both built by Norddeutscher Lloyd) and Cunard's *Mauritania* and *Lusitania*. In 1912, a White Star Line liner, the 'unsinkable' *Titanic*, sank after hitting an iceberg, resulting in the loss of 1,502 lives. In 1913, the *Imperator* (later renamed the *Berengaria*) became the first ship to exceed 50,000 tonnes gross weight.

Naval ships were also changing. The development of new weapons, such as the floating mine and the torpedo, meant that warships had to be constructed of something stronger than wood. By the early 1900s cruisers and heavily armoured battleships had been developed and the torpedo (invented in 1866) had led to the introduction of the torpedo boat and the torpedo boat destroyer. The first modern submarine, *Holland I*, had been built in the USA in 1897, and in 1905 the Germans developed their first *Unterseeboot*, or U-boat. In the same year, Enrico Forlanini built the first full-sized hydrofoil craft, which he tried out on Lake Maggiore in Italy.

Above The liner Celtic, being towed into port by a tug.

Below An artist's impression of the last moments of the Titanic, which sank in the North Atlantic in 1912, after colliding with an iceberg.

L'AÉRO-CLUB
DE FRANCE
PARIS

Certifie

ue M. *Wilbur*

Wright

a été nommé

PILOTE-AVIATEUR

e 7 Janvier 1909

LE PRESIDENT.

Into the air

In 1900, serious attempts at developing powered flying machines had been going on for over ten years. In 1890, a bat-like aircraft known as *Eole*, built by the Frenchman Clement Ader, had been the first powered aircraft to achieve a successful take-off. It 'hopped' a distance of 50 m. However, it was not until two American brothers, Wilbur and Orville Wright, worked out a way of controlling an aeroplane properly, that true powered flight was achieved. On 17 December 1903, Orville Wright flew the *Wright Flyer I* a distance of 36.5 m at Kill Devil Hills, North Carolina, in the USA. Later that day, Wilbur Wright flew 260 m, and two years later the brothers astounded the world with flights of over 30 km.

Left The French pilot's license issued to Wilbur Wright in 1909.

Below In 1906 Santos-Dumont made the first flight in Europe in his 14-bis.

Airships and gliders

Since early history people had dreamed of being able to copy the birds and use wings for flying. However, the first successful attempts at getting off the ground were made in hot air balloons. The Montgolfier brothers made the first manned flight in a balloon in France in 1783. In the same year, the gas balloon was invented by another Frenchman, Professor Jacques Charles. This, in turn, led to the development of many hydrogen-filled airships during the late 1800s and early 1900s, among which were the great German Zeppelins. Airship development was brought to an end during the 1930s, after several disasters. The R.101 crashed in 1930, killing forty-seven of the fifty-four people on board, and in 1936 the Hindenberg caught fire, killing thirty-five people.

Meanwhile, the dream of flying a heavier-than-air machine continued, and pioneers were having some success with gliders. In 1804, the British inventor Sir George Cayley worked out how wings lift a weight into the air. He and others, such as the German Otto Lilienthal and the American Octave Chanute, built a number of gliders in the 1800s. During the late 1800s, two American glider enthusiasts, Wilbur and Orville Wright, also built several gliders, incorporating a number of ideas for controlling the aircraft in flight. In 1903, they designed an engine and attached it to a new aeroplane, the Wright Flyer I. On 14 December Wilbur Wright tried this aircraft out, but crashed soon after take-off. The damage was repaired, and at 10.30 am on 17 December 1903, Orville Wright made history when he achieved the first controlled powered flight.

The first flight in Europe was made near Paris on 12 November 1906 by the Brazilian Alberto Santos-Dumont in his 14-*bis*. However, he and other European pilots, such as Gabriel Voisin, Henri Farman and Louis Blériot, were a long way behind the Wright brothers. In 1908, Henri Farman flew a Voisin-Farman I biplane a distance of 27 km. In 1909, Louis Blériot crossed the English Channel in a Blériot XI monoplane.

Aircraft development now proceeded very quickly. Speed became the most important design factor, and from 1909 to 1913 aircraft were mostly used for racing and in trials. Among the most famous aircraft designers of this time were Glen Curtiss in the USA, the American Samuel Cody, Alliot Roe, Geoffrey de Havilland, T.O.M. Sopwith and the Short brothers in Britain, and Anthony Fokker in Holland. In the USSR, Igor Sikorsky built the first four-engined aeroplane, the *Russkii Vitiaz*, which flew in 1913. In 1910, an American pilot, Eugene Ely was the first to use the combination of aircraft and ship when he took off from the USS *Birmingham* in a Curtiss biplane. The following year he succeeded in landing an aircraft on a cruiser.

Below A replica of Louis Blériot's Blériot XI, the first aeroplane to fly across the English Channel.

The Great War

The outbreak of the First World War had a dramatic effect on all forms of transport. With the war came the need for fighting machines and for fast methods of communication and supply.

Land transport

Transport has always been vital in time of war. The ability to move large numbers of soldiers, together with their weapons and supplies, is crucial during wartime. For thousands of years, the most important forms of transport had been the horse on land and wooden sailing ships at sea. However, when the First World War began, mechanized transport was starting to have a considerable influence upon the way in which wars were fought. Under the right conditions, troops could be moved rapidly to reinforce weak points in the front line. In 1914, 6,000 French troops were moved into Paris to repel the Germans. Communications were also speeded up by despatch riders on motorcycles, some of which were equipped with machine guns.

During the 1800s, railways had played a significant part in several wars. By the start of the First World War, there were armoured trains, heavy transporters and trains with guns permanently mounted on rail cars. But in the first few months of the war, the railway proved even more vital for moving supplies and troops.

In the summer of 1914, the war came to a standstill. Neither side could break through the line of trenches known as the Western Front, which stretched from Switzerland to the North Sea. The troops in these trenches needed vast quantities of supplies. The motorized transport that existed was not adequate for this task, and in any case, lorries frequently became stuck in the increasingly muddy conditions. The best

Below Motorcycles can travel over rough terrain. During the First World War they proved to be an excellent method of carrying messages.

Above German soldiers attempting to attack a British tank, temporarily stopped for repairs, during the Battle of the Somme in 1916.

Right British soldiers and nurses bound for France, leaving Victoria Station, London, in 1915.

solution to the problem proved to be light railways, and between 1914 and 1918, over 1,300 km of track were laid up to the Western Front. Over 1,200 locomotives were shipped over to Europe from Britain.

In 1915 a new form of fighting transport was devised by Lieutenant-Colonel Ernest Swinton. The tank, first used in the Battle of the Somme in 1916, enabled troops to cross difficult terrain into enemy territory.

War at sea and in the air

As on land, a new type of war was being fought at sea. Among the new kinds of warship were the Dreadnought type of battleship, which outclassed previous types. Even they were soon being threatened by the new German U-boats, which took a heavy toll of merchant shipping, until the convoy system was introduced.

At the outbreak of war, few people thought that air transport had much military importance. Aeroplanes were seen as being useful only for reconnaissance. Balloons and airships mostly had similar roles, although the German Zeppelins were used for bombing raids on Britain. Their success was due to poor British defences, and when the L.70 Zeppelin was brought down by a British seaplane in 1918, the bombing raids ceased immediately.

Aeroplanes soon began to change as the war in the air escalated. In 1915, the French aircraft, the Morane-Saulnier L, was fitted with a forward-firing machine gun. The German monoplane, the Fokker E III, or Eindekker, had a machine gun synchronized to fire in between the blades of the propeller. By the end of the war, both sides had a number of military aircraft, including reconnaissance aircraft, fighters, fighter bombers and bombers.

Above *A rigid airship on observation duty over a convoy during the First World War.*

Opposite page *In 1917 the British Sopwith Triplane, shown here in combat with a German Albatross D Va, outclassed all other fighter aircraft.*

Right *A German Fokker E III being displayed to an admiring crowd. A machine gun is mounted on its nose.*

Between the Wars

The First World War had provided valuable experience in the use of all forms of modern transport, and this was now employed more constructively. Cars became cheaper, aircraft began to carry passengers and liners continued to carry people and cargo around the world. The railways also continued to expand, although in the West they were beginning to lose business to the increasing road traffic.

The war had given considerable impetus to the development of the internal combustion engine. As a result, all forms of transport were modified and improved as petrol engines became more powerful and diesel engines were introduced. This process continued throughout the period between the wars, the only major setback being the depression of the early 1930s, which resulted in many companies going out of business.

Motoring for all

At the end of the war, demand for motor-cars increased and the motor industry underwent a rapid expansion. There was still a market for luxury motors, but now there was also an increasing demand for cheaper mass-produced cars. Among the most successful European cars in the 1920s were the Austin 7, or 'Baby Austin', and the Morris Cowley.

During the 1920s, many new features were added to cars. Engines with overhead camshafts were developed by companies with experience of aeroplane engines, such as Hispano-Suiza and Bentley. Four-wheel braking appeared, together with detachable wheels, all-steel bodies, windscreen wipers, electric starting and safety glass. Colour and style became more and more important as a selling point, and by 1930, saloon bodies,

Left *After the war products were advertised aggressively. This advertisement for Dunlop tyres was intended to appeal to people who liked the countryside.*

produce the KdF-Wagen, the Kraft durch Freude ('Strength through Joy') car, designed by Ferdinand Porsche. However, after 210 cars had been built, Hitler ordered the factory to switch to the production of military vehicles.

By the 1930s, lorries and buses had also been improved. Solid rubber tyres were being replaced with pneumatic ones, and diesel engines and articulated lorries were being introduced. Charabancs were being replaced by more comfortable motor-coaches.

Left The first Volkswagen 'Beetles' were built in 1938, but were not sold to the public until after the Second World War.

Below A 1935 petrol tanker.

cellulose paint and chromium plating had been introduced. The 1934 Citröen was the first to have a combined body and chassis, and was also the first car with front-wheel drive. In 1938 a German factory began to

Below The 1939 Plymouth was an American car with a folding outside rumble seat at the rear, to provide extra room for passengers.

Railways

Railways, which had proved so valuable during the war, continued to expand throughout the world. By 1930, some 1,100,000 km of track had been laid. Diesel-electric locomotives were first used in 1924, but for a time steam remained the most commonly used form of power. The largest locomotive ever built was the Union Pacific Mallet known as 'Big Boy', which weighed about 550 tonnes when fully loaded with water and fuel. In 1938, the streamlined British locomotive Mallard travelled at a speed of 202 kph, but by this time the end of the age of steam was in sight, and this remains the world speed record for a steam engine.

By the end of the 1930s it was clear that the heyday of the railways in Europe and the USA was also coming to an end, as railway companies began to face increasing competition from road vehicles.

Above The 4-6-0 steam locomotive 'Lord Nelson' first saw service in 1926 on Britain's Southern Railway. When it was built it was the most powerful locomotive in Britain.

The steam locomotive

Energy for a steam locomotive is provided by burning fuel in a firebox. This creates hot gases which are drawn from the firebox through narrow pipes, or flues, in a water-filled boiler. The heat from the flues turns the water to steam, which collects in the top of the boiler. From there it passes through a regulator valve to superheater pipes, in which the steam is heated to an even greater temperature and pressure. From there it is fed to each cylinder, first to one side of the piston and then the other, causing the piston to move to and fro. The pistons are linked to the wheels via a system of connecting rods, slide bars and cranks. Meanwhile, the exhaust steam passes out via the blast pipe and the chimney. As it leaves, it helps to draw more hot gas through the flues.

A steam locomotives is often described by a set of numbers (usually three) that indicates, in order, the number of front carrying wheels, the number of driving wheels and the number of rear carrying wheels. Common arrangements in the first half of the twentieth century included 4–4–0, 4–6–2 and 4–6–4.

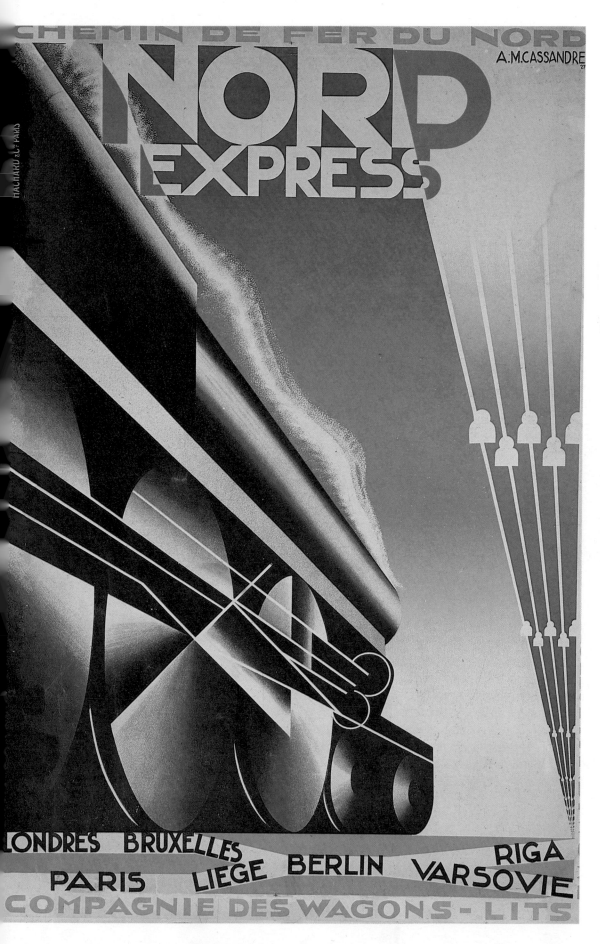

Left *A 1930s advertisement for the Nord Express. The Chemin de Fer du Nord (North railway) is one of the oldest in France; its origins date back to 1842. By the 1930s it was offering passengers a fast service to many important European cities.*

Passenger transport in the air

Above Alcock and Brown taking off from Newfoundland in their Vickers Vimy at the start of their historic flight across the Atlantic in 1919. They crash-landed in Derrygimla Bog, near Clifden, Ireland 16 hours 27 minutes later, having travelled 3,154 km.

Until 1918, aeroplanes had been limited to such uses as racing or combat, but after the war they began to be used as a genuine means of transport. Wartime bombers had proved that aircraft could carry heavy loads, and pioneer fliers now showed that long distance travel was possible. In 1919, John Alcock and Arthur Whitten Brown crossed the Atlantic in their Vickers Vimy aircraft. Powerful engines were now available, and a number of people began to see the possibilities of passenger transport. Airline services opened up in Germany, France and Britain, and the first international service was established by the British company Aircraft Transport and Travel. In 1919, this company opened services to France and Holland, using de Havilland D.H.4A aircraft modified from wartime bombers.

During the next twenty years, many new companies appeared. They often merged after a short time to form still larger airlines, such as Imperial Airways, British Airways, Air France, KLM, Deutsche Lufthansa, Transcontinental and Western Air (TWA) and Pan American (Pan Am). Many aircraft became famous throughout the world. Among these were the huge flying boats, such as Imperial Airways' Short S.8 Calcutta and Pan Am's Martin M-130 China Clipper. For many years Imperial Airways were best known for their Handley Page H.P.42s, but this and the equally well-known Boeing 80A were eventually superseded by all-metal, low-wing monoplanes, such as the Boeing 247 and the Douglas DC-2.

Smaller aircraft had also undergone considerable development. By the 1930s, there was a variety of fighters, racing aircraft and civil transporters. One of the most famous trainers of this time was the de Havilland D.H. 82A Tiger Moth. In 1927, Charles Lindbergh made the first solo non-stop crossing of the Atlantic in his Ryan NYP *Spirit of St Louis*. One year later, Charles Kingsford-Smith crossed the Pacific in his Fokker F VIIb-3m *Southern Cross*.

At the same time, engineers were developing a new type of engine – the gas turbine, or jet engine. In 1928, the British RAF pilot and engineer Frank Whittle published a paper on the subject, patenting his ideas two years later. By 1937, he had developed a successful prototype engine, but at this stage the British aviation industry showed little interest in his work. Meanwhile, a German, Pabst von Ohain, had begun studying the idea of a jet engine in 1935. His invention interested the aeroplane manufacturer Ernst von Heinkel, and a successful German engine was tested in 1937.

The jet engine was perhaps the most important invention in the field of transport in this period, although its implications for passenger travel could not be fully developed until the 1950s.

Above *The Westland Wizard was built in 1926 as a prototype fighter. In 1928 it took part in the RAF display at Hendon, but despite its early promise it was never put into production.*

Left *A de Havilland D.H.82A Tiger Moth. The first Tiger Moth flew in 1931 and a total of 7,300 were built.*

Carriers, diesel engines and hydrofoils

One of the major developments at the end of the First World War was the aircraft carrier. Torpedo-carrying seaplanes that took off from ships at sea had been used during the war, but the development of the true carrier came too late to take part. In 1919, Britain launched HMS *Hermes*, the first ship designed and built as a carrier. By the 1930s, the world's navies had a number of huge carriers, some of which could carry over eighty aircraft.

Steam power still dominated the world's shipping at the end of the war. However, diesel power was gaining ground, and the first diesel-engined passenger vessel, the 18,281 tonne *Gripsholm* was built in Sweden in 1925. By 1930, over half of the new ships being built were powered by diesel engines.

Meanwhile, the hydrofoil was also making progress. In 1927, the German engineer Baron Hans von Schertel designed the V-foil, which meant that a hydrofoil was stable in fairly rough weather. Ten years later the Köln-Düsseldorf Steamship Company placed the first commercial order for one of von Schertel's craft. By this time, the depression was ending, and in 1934 the magnificent liner the *Queen Mary* was launched. She carried up to 2,000 passengers and could cross the Atlantic in just over four days.

The Second World War

The war in Europe and the Far East provided a sense of urgency to the improvements already being made to transport. Fighting machines of all kinds developed rapidly, but aircraft in particular revolutionized warfare.

War on land

The motorcar changed little during the Second World War. Few cars were produced, as most of the materials were needed for military use, and petrol became very scarce throughout Europe. Motorcycles became increasingly popular. Some buses and lorries were converted to run on producer-gas; the fuel was stored in a trailer towed behind the vehicle.

Towards the end of the 1930s, as war seemed more and more inevitable, the production of military lorries had been increased. Many were just militarized versions of commercial lorries, although there

Right A German motorcycle patrol in the North African desert. As in the First World War, motorcycles proved to be useful all-terrain vehicles.

Left and below The German advance into the Soviet Union in 1942 was carried out using road vehicles. Officers travelled in cars and troops travelled in convoys of lorries escorted by motorcyclists. Artillery (below) was also brought up by land.

were a number of specialized vehicles, such as artillery tractors and tank transporters. Other military vehicles included staff cars and a general-purpose four-wheel drive vehicle known as the GP, or 'jeep', of which there were a number of versions, including an amphibious type.

The railways were less important in the Second World War than they had been in the 1914–18 war. However, they were used to advantage on many occasions, and the Germans in particular preferred to move troops and equipment in this way. The British and Americans, on the other hand, relied more upon road transport.

Above HMS Benbow with the British Second Battle Squadron.

War at sea

In many ways the war at sea followed a similar pattern to the course of the First World War. The Germans tried hard to prevent merchant ships from carrying supplies between the USA, Britain and the USSR, and the Allies tried equally hard to keep these vital shipping lanes open. The Germans had highly efficient submarines, or U-boats, that sank many ships during the early years of the war. Midget submarines were used by the British and Japanese, and all the fighting nations had a variety of surface warships, including, battleships, cruisers, destroyers, torpedo boats, motor-gunboats, minelayers and minesweepers. Aircraft carriers really proved their usefulness during the Second World War.

Right The view towards the stern from the conning tower of a German U-boat. U-boats sank a great deal of merchant shipping during the Second World War.

War in the air

In the First World War aircraft had proved to be of some help to ground forces. In the Second World War, air support was vital to both sea and land forces, and the aeroplane became a tactical weapon in its own right. In 1940, the *Luftwaffe* failed to gain control of the air during the Battle of Britain, and the German invasion of England had to be postponed. A few years later, strategic bombing of Germany played a key role in the eventual Allied victory.

By the beginning of the war, sleek all-metal monoplane fighters were replacing the old biplanes. The *Luftwaffe* had 1,200 fighters in 1939, including the well-known Messerschmitt Bf 109, which outclassed all other fighters. The British RAF had far fewer aircraft, but in spite of this disadvantage, heavy losses were inflicted by squadrons of Supermarine Spitfires and Hawker Hurricanes on German bombers over Britain.

Other fighters that played important roles during the war included Britain's multi-role de Havilland Mosquito, Germany's Focke-Wulf Fw 190, the American Lockheed P-38 Lightning and the Japanese Mitsubishi A6M2 Reisen. The RAF also had the Bristol Beaufighter, which was equipped with an early form of radar for intercepting other aircraft at night.

Among the strategic bombers used by the Allies were Britain's Vickers Wellington and Avro Lancaster. The Americans had the Boeing B-17 Flying Fortress and the Consolidated B-24 Liberator, of which 18,000 were built. German pilots flew the Heinkel He III, the Dornier Do 217 and the multi-role Junkers Ju 88, the *Luftwaffe's* equivalent of the Mosquito.

Meanwhile, the Russian–American aircraft designer Igor Sikorsky had developed the first practical helicopter, the VS-316A, which flew in 1942. At the same time, the jet engine was making progress. In 1939, the Heinkel He 178 was the first jet aircraft to take to the air. In Britain, the first jet aeroplane was an experimental Gloster, the E.28/39, which flew in 1941, and the Gloster Meteor, which first flew in March 1943. One

Below *The Focke-Wulf 190A-1 went into service in 1941 and proved to be the best German fighter of the Second World War.*

Left *A view inside a Halifax, one of the outstanding British bombers that played a crucial role in the Second World War.*

Centre *The German city of Bremen after it was bombed by the Allies.*

year later, the Meteor was brought into service in Britain, and the Messerschmitt Me 262 was used in Germany.

The development of the gas turbine (jet) engine during the 1930s and 1940s affected more than one form of transport. The first gas turbine railway locomotive had been introduced on to the Swiss Federal Railways in 1941. Soon after the war, there were ships powered by gas turbine engines, and even one or two experimental gas turbine cars. However, the greatest effect was upon the development of aircraft.

The Jet Age

In the ten years after the war, aircraft powered by jet engines rapidly became very common. On land, the number of cars began to increase, and as a result the railways in many parts of the world declined. At sea, ships became more specialized.

Below *An F-100 Super Sabre of the United States Air Force, the first plane to fly faster than the speed of sound.*

The gas turbine engine

A gas turbine engine works by drawing in air, which is then compressed and heated. The hot, compressed air passes into the combustion chambers, where the fuel is injected in a constant stream. The fuel burns and expands, forcing its way out through the turbine, which also consists of several sets of blades. The turbine drives the compressor, but only some of the energy contained in the hot gas is used up in doing this. The remaining energy can be used to produce forward thrust or to drive a third set of blades, the power fan, which can be attached to a piece of machinery, such as a ship's propeller.

The simplest form of jet engine is the turbojet, which is a gas turbine engine with a nozzle at the rear to provide jet propulsion. This was the type of engine devised by Frank Whittle. A turbojet is noisy and inefficient at low speeds, but these problems are reduced in a turboprop engine. In this, the turbine has more sets of blades, which take up more energy from the escaping hot gases. This energy is then transferred, via a gear box and shaft, to a propeller at the front of the engine.

Modern airliners are powered by turbofan engines. In this type of engine, the turbine drives an extra low-speed fan rather than a propeller. The fan acts like a large compressor, and the air it compresses is divided into two parts. One part enters the compressor, as it does in a turbojet; the remainder flows round the outside of the engine casing, helping to cool the engine and reduce noise. Turbofan engines produce a greater thrust at low speeds than turbojets, and are more efficient at high speeds than turboprops.

Jet aircraft

Jet engines were developed during this period mainly in the USA, USSR, Britain and France. The engines built at the beginning of the war had produced between 500 and 1,000 kg of thrust, but by 1949 there were engines that could generate ten times as much power as this. By the mid-1950s, piston-engined aircraft had become completely outdated.

Gas turbine engines also proved to be ideal for turning the rotor shafts of helicopters, which demonstrated their usefulness during the Korean War. The first jet airliner was the de Havilland D.H.106 Comet I, which entered service in May 1952. In 1953, a North American F-100 Super Sabre became the first jet aircraft to fly faster than the speed of sound. In 1954, Rolls-Royce successfully used the 'flying bedstead' – an experimental test-bed for vertical take-off.

Left Passengers boarding the world's first regular jetliner service, between London and Johannesburg, South Africa, in May 1952.

Specialist ships

The first ship powered by a gas turbine engine was a motor gunboat, MGB 2009. However, diesel engines had now become the most common form of propulsion for smaller ships; only larger vessels continued to use steam turbines. In 1954, the world's first nuclear-powered vessel, the US Navy submarine *Nautilus*, was launched. Instead of oil or coal, a nuclear reactor generated the heat needed to produce steam for the turbines.

By 1945, much of the world's merchant and naval shipping had been sunk, or damaged beyond repair. However, the process of rebuilding that now began gave shipping lines the opportunity of building more specialist ships – ships designed for particular tasks. A few specialist ships had existed since the mid-1800s; for example, the first oil tanker had been launched in 1856, and many other cargo ships had been modified to carry particular cargos. However, during the ten years after the Second World War the numbers of these ships increased.

Above *The nuclear-powered US submarine* Nautilus *arriving at Portland, Dorset in the UK after crossing the North Pole underneath the icecap in 1958.*

Right *During the 1950s the Orient Line offered travellers voyages to Australia via the Suez Canal.*

Postwar cars

After the Second World War, European car manufacturers began producing cars again, in spite of the fact that materials were often in short supply. Demand for cars was high, even though petrol and replacement tyres were also difficult to obtain. Many of these new European cars had independent front suspension, and disc brakes became more widely used. In the USA, the tubeless tyre and automatic transmission were introduced. Radial tyres appeared in 1953, and glass fibre panels were first used on the 1953 Chevrolet Corvette and the 1955 Citröen DS19. A few manufacturers tried to develop gas turbine engines for use in cars, but these were not a success.

Above A 1946 Morris 10.

Above *The 1947 Oldsmobile was typical of the large, heavily styled American postwar cars.*

In Europe, one of the most successful cars was the German KdF-Wagen, by now renamed the Volkswagen, whose basic shape has remained virtually unchanged to this day. Since the factory reopened in 1945, over 20 million VWs have been sold.

Another well-known car was the Jaguar XK-120, one of the classic sports cars. This model first appeared in 1948, the same year as the Morris Minor and the Citröen 2CV.

In America, a few large corporations, such as Ford, Chrysler and General Motors, now began to dominate the motor manufacturing market, and cars were beginning to lose their individualistic appearance. This was the era of cars with huge front grilles and large panels of bright chrome and plastic.

Above *The Jaguar XK 120, first produced in 1948, became one of the world's best known classic cars.*

Postwar railways

In 1945, in the parts of Europe hardest hit by the war, the railways were in a very poor state. Nevertheless, a programme of rebuilding progressed rapidly, and many lines were electrified. In France, where the railways had suffered less devastation than elsewhere, SNCF (*Société Nationale de Chemins de Fers*) continued to expand the network of electrified railways that had been started after the First World War. In Britain, the four largest railway companies were amalgamated in 1948 to form the nationalized company British Railways. The decision to phase out steam locomotives in Britain was not taken until 1955, and then the replacements were to be mainly diesel-electric. Other decisions taken at this time meant that Britain's railways became one of the least efficient systems in Europe.

Nothing, however, could prevent the inevitable decline of the railways due to competition from road traffic. The Second World War had temporarily postponed this decline, but now it continued, particularly in the USA where railway traffic had been gradually decreasing since 1916.

Left *A 1950s advertisement extolling the virtues of travelling to the Côte d'Azur (the French Mediterranean coast) by train.*

The Space Age

The launching of the first satellite heralded the start of a new era. Millions of television viewers watched in amazement when Neil Armstrong took the first step on the Moon in 1969. Meanwhile, on Earth, air transport rapidly increased, resulting in a decrease in demand for transport at sea. On land, many more people became car owners and the railways were brought up to date.

Rockets

The modern liquid-fuelled rocket was devised by the American scientist Robert Goddard in 1909. His first rocket reached a height of 12.5 m. During the Second World War, the German scientist Wernher von Broun developed the first long-range rocket, known as the V2, which was used to bombard London and Antwerp from launch sites in the Netherlands. After the war, German scientists in both the USA and the USSR helped to develop a range of increasingly powerful rockets. The largest rockets ever built were the huge Saturn rockets used to launch the Apollo spacecraft. Modern rockets include Ariane (Europe), Proton (USSR) and Titan (USA).

The principle on which a rocket works is based on Newton's third law of motion – for every action there is an equal and opposite reaction. Thus, the action of forcing a jet of hot gas out of the rear of a rocket engine produces a forward motion in the rocket itself. The rocket is not, as some people imagine, propelled forward by the gases pushing against the air – the principle works equally well in space, where there is no air.

The fuel used in a modern rocket is usually liquid hydrogen, which is stored in a tank. Oxygen is needed to burn the fuel and this is supplied by the rocket itself, in the form of liquid oxygen from a second tank. The hydrogen and oxygen are pumped to a combustion chamber, where the fuel is ignited by a spark or hot wire. The expanding hot exhaust gases escape through a nozzle at the rear of the engine, propelling the rocket forward faster than the speed of sound.

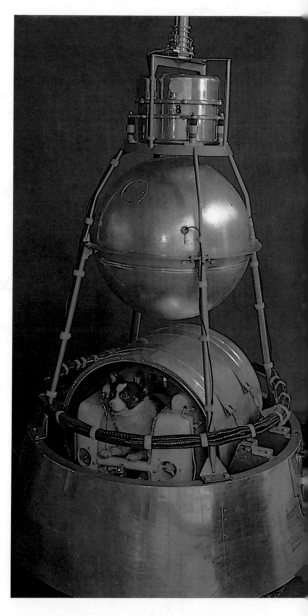

The spacecraft Sputnik 2 which carried the first living creature, the dog Laika, into space in November 1957.

Photographed by Neil Armstrong, Edwin Aldrin steps from the Apollo 11 *lunar module on to the surface of the Moon on 20 July 1969.*

On 4 October 1957, the USSR launched the spacecraft *Sputnik 1*. Its load was small – just a radio that transmitted a series of bleeps back to Earth – but it showed that objects could be transported into space. One month later, a dog named Laika was launched into space in *Sputnik 2*, and on 12 April, 1961, the Russian pilot Yuri Gagarin became the first space traveller, or cosmonaut, when he orbited the Earth once in his spacecraft *Vostok 1*.

The next major goal was a landing on the Moon. Determined to get there first, the Americans began launching a series of manned spacecraft named Apollo. On 21 July 1969, watched by millions of television viewers, Neil Armstrong and Edwin ('Buzz') Aldrin stepped off the *Apollo 11* lunar module on to the Moon's surface. Between then and 1972, five more Apollo missions landed on the Moon. After the Moon landings came to an end, manned space flight continued nearer Earth. In 1971, the USSR launched the first space station, *Salyut 1*, and the USA launched *Skylab* in 1973.

The Soviets have tended to concentrate on robotic spacecraft. Using their highly successful *Luna* probes, they succeeded in landing Lunokhod roving vehicles and bringing back samples of Moon rock. The Americans and Soviets have also used robotic spacecraft to study planets of our solar system by sampling their atmospheres and taking photographs of their surfaces.

Above A Boeing 747 coming in to land at Heathrow Airport, London.

Air travel for all

From the late 1950s onwards, air travel became more popular. Freight was being carried by aircraft, and many new airlines were being started up. They began to build up fleets of large jet airliners. Among the most successful were the Boeings, beginning with the Boeing 707 in 1958. In 1970, Pan Am introduced into their fleet the Boeing 747, the first Jumbo airliner, capable of carrying 500 passengers. Concorde, the world's first supersonic airliner, made its first flight in 1969 and was brought into service in 1976. This aircraft made it possible to cross the Atlantic in just three hours.

Military aircraft were also becoming increasingly sophisticated. The success of the Rolls-Royce 'flying bedstead' led to the development of the Hawker Siddeley Harrier, the first VTOL (vertical take-off and landing) aircraft. Helicopters were proving their versatility, and the helicopter gunship was first used in the Vietnam war. Fighters and bombers were built with swept-back wings, as speeds increased, and the variable-geometry, or swing-wing, design was introduced into supersonic aircraft, such as the American Rockwell B1 bomber and the French Dassault G.8 fighter.

A new form of transport was also invented during this period. In 1959, Sir Christopher Cockerell designed the first workable hovercraft, a vehicle supported on a cushion of air. Since then, hovercraft have been used as a form of high-speed transport over water, and across surfaces that other forms of transport find difficult, such as swampy ground and ice.

Right *The American Bell UH-1 'Huey', first produced in 1956, became one of the world's most famous helicopters during the war in Vietnam.*

Below *At present, Concorde remains the only supersonic airliner in service.*

Giant ships and nuclear power

The increase in passenger air travel in the late 1950s resulted in a simultaneous decline in the number of passengers who wanted to travel by sea. By the 1970s, liners had become cruise ships, catering for the holiday-maker rather than the traveller. At the same time, the number of specialized cargo ships was increasing. When the Suez Canal closed during the Arab–Israeli war of 1967, shipbuilders began building even larger cargo ships. Supertankers for carrying oil round the Cape of Good Hope came first, followed by other bulk-cargo vessels and,

finally, container ships. The British container ship *Euroliner*, launched in 1971, was the first to be powered by gas turbines. The first LASH (Lighter Aboard Ship) vessel was built in 1969.

The first nuclear-powered cargo vessel was the American merchant ship *Savannah*, launched in 1958, followed by the Soviet icebreaker *Lenin*, which was commissioned in 1959. However, nuclear power was not a popular energy source for merchant ships and after this the only nuclear-powered vessels built were warships and submarines.

Opposite page *A cargo ship carrying tanks and other military equipment.*

Below *The cruise ship* Royale *at Nassau in the Bahamas.*

Family cars and high speed trains

The number of cars on the roads continued to increase, as family motoring became more popular. At the same time, competition between car manufacturers was very strong and many motor companies disappeared, often as the result of mergers with other organizations. One of the outstanding cars of the period was the Mini Minor, first produced by the British Motor Corporation (BMC) in 1959. Other memorable cars of the era include the Triumph TR series, the MGA, the Citröen DS and the Mercedes 300SL coupé. By the 1970s, the design of cars had changed to squared-off edges and corners rather than rounded surfaces, and three- or five-door hatchbacks were introduced. Fuel economy became more important, particularly after the oil crisis of 1973, with the result that small cars became increasingly popular.

The amount of traffic carried by the railways continued to decline, and in order to stay in business, railway companies had to rationalize and modernize their systems. In 1963 a report by Lord Beeching recommended developing the railways as freight carriers and closing many small branch lines. As a result, the amount of railway track in Britain was reduced from 32,600 km to 18,500 km, most of which linked major cities. During the 1970s, parts of the track were electrified, and high-speed intercity diesel-electric trains were introduced.

Elsewhere in the world, other fast train services were also achieving success. In Japan, the Tokaido line was opened in 1964 between Tokyo and Osaka. Electric *Shinkansen Hikari*, or 'lightning trains' ran every fifteen minutes, and the line has since been extended to run the full length of the islands that make up Japan. Turbo-trains, with electric motors powered by gas-turbine engines, started to be used in Canada and France during the 1970s.

Shuttles and Robots

The modern electronics industry has played a large part in the development of modern transport, and there is an increasing tendency towards using robot transport of all kinds. At the same time, the need to economize on fuel and materials, and to reduce environmental pollution, is affecting the design of today's vehicles.

Above *The launch of the American space shuttle* Discovery *in September 1988.*

LASH vessels
The system known as lighter aboard ship is a method of loading and unloading a ship without the ship having to enter a dock. Goods are loaded aboard lighters (barges) and then floated out to the ship. Early forms of LASH vessels loaded the barges using complex lifting gear, which was inclined to break down and cause delays. Modern LASH vessels can be lowered in the water to allow the barges to be floated on and off the deck.

When the Apollo Moon programme came to an end, the Americans began, once again, to concentrate on projects closer to Earth. In 1981, they launched the space shuttle, which was the first reusable spacecraft, and for a few years this was successful, carrying a variety of satellites into Earth's orbit. In 1986, however, the space shuttle *Challenger* exploded in mid-air soon after being launched, killing all seven people on board. This and other accidents resulted in a long delay in the American space programme, although it got underway again with the successful launching of the space shuttle *Discovery* on 29 September 1988. Meanwhile, the USSR has been making slower but steady progress, and an unmanned Soviet space shuttle was launched on 15 November 1988. As well as launching satellites and space probes, shuttles in the future may be used to help build laboratories and solar power stations in space.

The increasing sophistication of spacecraft and satellites owes much to the recent advances made in the electronics industry. Similar changes have occurred in air transport, and many modern aircraft are equipped with computers that can assist in take-off, landing, flying and navigation. As well as bombers and fighters, military aircraft now include a new intermediate type known as the attack aircraft. Tilt- rotor aircraft, which can take off like a helicopter and then fly like a conventional aeroplane, are also beginning to be used. As yet, Concorde remains the only supersonic passenger aircraft in service. However, future supersonic transporters may be boosted high into the sky, flying for part of the time outside the Earth's

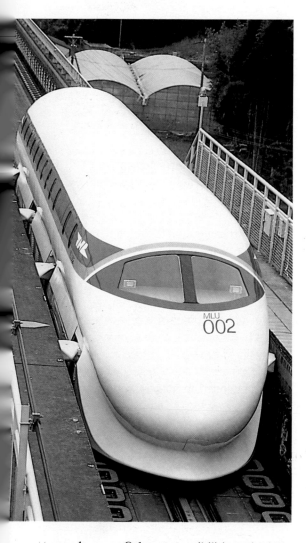

atmosphere. Other possibilities include helium-filled airships and huge airliners.

As the world's population increases, efficient land transport is becoming vital. The motorcar remains popular, but it is one of the least efficient methods of transport, and pollution from vehicle exhausts is a rapidly growing problem. Inner-city transport is increasingly being provided by electric trains, above and below ground, and in some places, driverless, robot trains now operate. People movers, (small-tracked cabins), are already in use in such places as airports, and in the future this form of transport may replace the motorcar in cities.

In some parts of the world, such as China and India, railways are still dependent upon steam. In more highly developed countries, most railways operate either electric or diesel-electric locomotives, although some steam railways have been preserved by enthusiasts. The world's fastest modern train is the French *TGV* (*Turbotrain à Grande Vitesse*), which has a top speed of 270 kph. In the future, some trains may be supported by magnetic levitation instead of running on rails.

Economy is also an increasingly important factor in sea transport. The Japanese tanker *Shin-Aitoku-Maru*, launched in 1980, is equipped with rigid sails. These are automatically set by a computer and can help save a large amount of fuel on a long journey. In future we may see more LASH vessels, and a similar type of ship known as the 'bacat' (barge aboard catamaran). Nuclear-powered submarine transporters could be used to carry large heavy loads over long distances. Modern satellite navigation systems, linked to on-board and shore-based computers, may enable future transport ships to be sailed without crews.

Above Airship Industrie's Skyship 500, shown here linked to its ground support vehicle. Airships may play an increasingly important role in future transport.

Above left Testing the Japanese MLU-002 maglev (magnetic levitation) train.

Glossary

Astronaut   A traveller in space, literally a 'star sailor'.

Battleship   A heavily armed warship, designed to defeat all other forms of warship.

Camshaft   A revolving shaft which operates the valves of an internal combustion engine.

Carburettor   A device for delivering a mixture of air and vaporized fuel to the cylinder of a petrol-driven piston engine. Fuel is vaporized as it is mixed with air, and is delivered to the cylinder via an inlet valve.

Convoy system   A system in which merchant ships travelled together in convoys protected by warships.

Cosmonaut   The Soviet name for an astronaut.

Crankshaft   The main shaft of an internal combustion engine.

Cruiser   A warship designed for speed.

Destroyer   Abbreviated form of 'torpedo-boat destroyer'. The destroyer became so successful that by 1965 it had replaced the cruiser.

Diesel-electric locomotive   A type of railway locomotive in which the driving power is provided by electricity supplied from batteries. A powerful diesel engine drives a generator to supply electric power to the batteries.

Diesel engine   An engine in which fuel oil is ignited by being injected into hot, compressed air.

Disc brake   A form of brake in which a rotating disc attached to the wheel shaft is gripped by a pair of brake pads in order to slow it down. (In the most common alternative system, known as a drum brake, two pistons force a pair of curved brake shoes outwards so that they make contact with the inside of a drum.)

Gas turbine   An engine in which burning fuel produces hot expanding exhaust gases that are then used to drive a turbine.

Hovercraft   A vehicle supported on a cushion of air. The air cushion is produced by one or more powerful fans and is contained within a flexible skirt around the base of the craft.

Hydrofoil   A ship or boat equipped with one or more underwater aerodynamically shaped foils. The foils act like wings and lift the craft out of the water as it gains forward speed.

Internal combustion engine   An engine in which fuel is burned inside the cylinders, in contrast to a steam engine in which fuel is burned in a separate furnace.

LASH vessels   A lighter aboard ship can be loaded and unloaded without entering port by floating barges containing cargo on and off the deck.

Magnetic levitation   A method of lifting a vehicle off a track, using two strong magnetic fields – one on the track and one on the vehicle itself. The fields repel each other and the train floats above the track.

Phaeton   A high, four-wheeled carriage, normally drawn by one or two horses.

Producer-gas   A gas mixture, containing the flammable gases hydrogen and carbon monoxide, produced by passing air over hot coke.

Radiator   A device used for reducing the temperature of the water in an engine's cooling system. The water passes through many narrow channels, which are equipped with vanes to increase the surface area through which cooling can take place.

Reconnaissance   The process of obtaining information about the position and strength of the enemy and of possible targets.

Satellite   Any object, such as a moon, that orbits a large planet. Orbiting spacecraft are artificial, or man-made, satellites.

Shuttle   Any vehicle that travels regularly to and fro between two points.

Supersonic   Faster than the speed of sound.

Tanker   A ship, aeroplane or lorry designed for carrying large quantities of liquid.

Torpedo   A self-propelled cylindrical weapon that can be launched from a ship, submarine or aircraft.

Transmission   The system of gears and shafts used for taking power from an engine to the driving wheels of a motor vehicle.

Turbine   A machine in which energy in a moving fluid, such as water or hot air, produces rotational movement in a set of blades attached to a central shaft.

U-boat   Abbreviation of *Unterseeboot*, the German word for submarine.

Further Reading

Angelucci, Enzo, and Matricardi, Paolo, **World Aircraft** (Sampson Low 1977).

Burgess-Wise, David, **The Illustrated History of Road Transport** (New Burlington Books 1986).

Haws, Duncan, **Ships and the Sea** (Chancellor Press 1985).

Kerrod, Robin, **Just Look at . . . Space Exploration** (Macdonald Educational 1984).

Lambert, Mark, **Transport in the Future** (Wayland 1986).

Lambert, Mark, and Insley, Jane, **Communications and Transport** 1986).

Mondy, David, (Ed) **The International Encyclopedia of Aviation** (Octopus Books 1977).

Nock, O.S., (Ed) **Encyclopedia of Railways** (Octopus Books 1977).

Taylor, Ron, and Lambert, Mark, **The Mechanical World** (Macdonald Educational 1979).

Wyatt, Robert **The World of Transport** (Macdonald Educational 1976).

Picture acknowledgements

The illustrations in this book were supplied by: BBC Hulton Picture Library 8, 13 (below), 17 (above left), 22; The Bridgeman Art Library 7, 15, 16, 19, 21 (above), 29, 32 (below); Camera Press 12, 14 (above), 26, 27, 28–9; Mary Evans Picture Library *back cover*; The Mansell Collection 9 (below), 10 (above and below), 13 (above), 20; Peter Newark 30–31; Science Photo Library 36 (Novosti), 37 (NASA), 38 (Martin Bond) 42–3 (Phil Jade), 44 (NASA), 45 left (Takeshi Takahara) and right (Alex Bartel); Topham, *title page*, 5 (above and below), 6 (above and below), 9 (above), 14 (below), 23 (main picture and inset), 24, 25 (above and below), 28, 31, 32 (above), 35, 39 (above), 43; Zefa Picture Library *front cover*, 11 (J. Sedlmeier), 17 (right and below), 18, 21, (below), 34 above (I. Seiff), below (D. Cattani), 39 (below), 40, 41.

Index

(Page numbers for illustrations are in *italics*.)

Ader, Clement   10
Aeroplanes   10–11, 44
 freight   38
 jet   21, 28–9, 30–31, *30–31*, 38
 military   14, *15*, 20, *21*, 22, 28,
   28, *29*, 38, 44
 passenger 20–21, *31*, 38, *38*, *39*,
   40
 seaplanes   22
 tilt-rotor   44
Airlines   20, 38
Airships   14, *14*, 45
Alcock, John   20, *20*
Aldrin, Edwin   37
Armstrong, Neil   37
Austin   6, 16

Balloons   14
Bentley   16
Benz, Karl   4
Blériot, Louis   11
Boeing   38, *38*
BMC   42
Brown, Arthur Whitten   20, *20*
Buses   6, *6*, 17, 24

Cars: *see* Motorcars
Charabancs   6, 17
Chevrolet   33
Chrysler   34
Citröen   17, 33, 34, 42
Cockerell, Sir Christopher   39
Cody, Samuel   11
Curtiss, Glen   11
Cyclecar   6

Daimler, Gottlieb   4, *5*
De Dion Bouton   4
Duryea   4

Ely, Eugene   11

Farman, Henri   11
First World War   11, 12–15
Fokker   11
Ford, Henry   6

Ford Motor Company   6–7, 34
Forlanini, Enrico   9

Gagarin, Yuri   37
General Motors   34

Havilland, Geoffrey de   11, 31
Hawker Siddeley Harrier   38
Heinkel, Ernst von   21
Helicopters   28, 30, 38, *39*
Hispano-Suiza   16
Hovercraft   39
Hydrofoils   9, 22

Jaguar   34, *34*
Jeep   25

KdF-Wagen: *see* Volkswagen
Kingsford-Smith, Charles   21

Lanchester   4
Levassor   4
Lindbergh, Charles   *20*, 21
Locomotives   12
 diesel   8
 diesel-electric   18, 35, 43
 electric   8
 gas-turbine (jet)   29
 high-speed   43, *43*, 45
 robot   45
 steam   8, *8*, 18, *18*, 35, 45
Lorries   12, 17
 military   12, 24–5, *25*
 producer-gas-powered   24

Mallet and Garatt   8
Mercedes   4, 42
Morris   6, 16, 34
Motorcars   4–7, 16, 24, 33–4, 42,
   45
 diesel   16
 fuel economy   42
 military   12, *12*, 25, *25*
 petrol   16, 24, 33
 three-wheeled   4
Motorcycles   6, 12, *12*, 24, *24*, *25*

Napier   6

Ohain, Pabst von   21

Panhard   4

Parsons, Sir Charles   9
Petrol tanker   *17*
Peugeot   4
Porsche, Ferdinand   7

Railways   4, 8, *8*, 12, *19*, 25, 35,
   35, 43
 electric   35, 43
Roe, Alliot   11
Rolls-Royce   6, *21*, 31, 38

Santos-Dumont, Alberto   *10*, 11
Schertel, Hans von   22
Second World War   24–9, 36
Ships   4
 cargo   32, *41*
 container   40
 cruise   40
 diesel-powered   9, 22
 gas-turbine (jet)   32, 40
 LASH   40, 44, 45
 merchant   26
 naval   9, 14, 22, *22*, 26, *26*
 nuclear-powered   40
 oil tanker   32, 40
 passenger   22, *22*, *32*
 steam-powered   9, 22, 32
Short brothers   11
Sikorsky, Igor   11, 28
Sopwith, T. O. M.   11
Spacecraft
 Apollo   37, *37*
 space shuttles   44, *44*
 Sputnik   *36*, 37
Submarines   9, 14, 26, *27*
 nuclear-powered   32, *32*, 45
Swinton. Ernest   11

Tanks   13, *13*
Tyres   5, *16*, 17, 33

Voisin, Gabriel   11
Volkswagen   17, *17*, 34

Whittle, Frank   21
Wright brothers   10–11, *10*

Zeppelin   11, 14